Just the Right
Christmas
WORDS

Just the Right Christmas WORDS

JUDITH WIBBERLEY

D&C
David and Charles

In loving memory of
GERTRUDE WIBBERLEY
A loving grandmother, who encouraged me to become a writer

A DAVID & CHARLES BOOK
Copyright © David & Charles Limited 2009

David & Charles is an F+W Media Inc. company
4700 East Galbraith Road
Cincinnati, OH 45236

Text copyright © Judith Wibberley 2009
Layout and Illustrations copyright
© David & Charles 2009

Reprinted in 2010

A catalogue record for this book is available
from the British Library.
ISBN-13: 978-0-7153-3155-2 hardback
ISBN-10: 0-7153-3155-8 hardback

ISBN-13: 978-0-7153-3156-9 paperback
ISBN-10: 0-7153-3156-6 paperback

Printed in Singapore by KHL Printing Co Pte Ltd
for David & Charles
Brunel House, Newton Abbot, Devon

Commissioning Editor: Bethany Dymond
Editorial Assistant: James Brooks
Designer and Illustrator: Mia Farrant
Project Editor: Ann Plume
Production Controller: Kelly Smith

David & Charles publish high quality books on a
wide range of subjects.
For more great book ideas visit:
www.rucraft.co.uk

Contents

Acknowledgments

My thanks to Bethany Dymond and her team at David & Charles, publishers who have created a beautiful third book of verses, sentiments and sayings from my original words. My heartfelt thanks to those who loved the previous two books so much that you made this third one possible for me.

My love, as always, to my husband Colin, my knight in shining armour, who fills my life with so much joy, inspiration, support and love. All of this and more is also provided by my daughter Deborah, who was my proof reader, my son James, my daughter-in-law Angela, my lovely grandson Luke and my beautiful granddaughter Katie. May they always know that I love them more than any of my words could ever convey.

These verses are also inspired by the treasured family who I have loved and lost but moreover by those who have been exceptional friends throughout my life and to true angels who have touched my life in so many ways and walked with me. True friendship is such a precious gift from God and I thank Him for colouring my life with a beautiful rainbow of friends who brought me love and support, especially my good friend and business partner, Deborah Murphy.

Christmas is a magical time for me and holds many treasured memories over the years that I have shared with my family, children, grandchildren and good friends. All of these moments and past reflections are woven into these original words written especially for all of you.

> "The only blind person at Christmastime is he who has not Christmas in his heart."
> HELEN KELLER (1880-1968)

Introduction

A seasonal collection of original verses, sentiments, sayings and copyright-free motifs especially for card makers, paper crafters and for those who wish to add a personal touch to an otherwise blank card. This third book of original verses is another invaluable point of reference for your card crafting and greeting needs at Christmas. Amongst these charming and witty verses you will find poignant verses for your loved ones, written straight from the heart, with words that were inspired by treasured moments spent with dear friends and close relatives who made Christmas a magical time for the author. There are special words for Advent, Christmas and New Year invitations, letters to Santa, a celebration of winter weddings, Christmas birthdays, Baby's 1st Christmas, remembering those in the forces or living overseas, and holiday sentiments. All are designed to bring the final touch of elegance and expression to your work by adding thoughts, feelings and emotions not found in cards produced for the mass market.

May these heartfelt Christmas words remind you of the five principles of the Advent candles: the first a candle of **hope**, the second a candle of **peace**, the third a candle of **love**, the fourth a candle of **joy**, and the fifth a candle that represents **the birth of Jesus Christ**. The candle flames remind us that He is the light of the world bringing us out of the darkness. At Christmas, nothing should overshadow the birth of Christ, God's ultimate gift. May you use these words in such a way that they echo around the world making people smile because they know that they are truly loved and in the thoughts of caring friends and family at this special time of year when God gave the world the gift of **love**.

Countdown to Christmas

As Christmas comes ever near
Remember why this time is here

As Christmas approaches
Think how you can make
The world brighter for those
Who are living in the shadows
Bring peace, harmony and love

*Each day of Advent
Remember the reason
We give thanks to God
For this marvellous season*

𝒴ou are the only star I want to
follow this Christmas

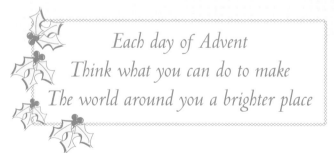

Each day of Advent
Think what you can do to make
The world around you a brighter place

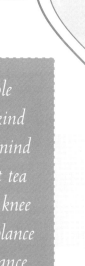

Listen to angels singing on high
As the birth of Jesus draws ever nigh

During Advent give people
A smile or two, a gesture kind
A listening ear, thoughtful mind
A special brew of your best tea
And cuddles sat upon your knee
Kind words or a knowing glance
Time to reflect, a second chance
A pat on the back for good cheer
Spread love around, Advent's here

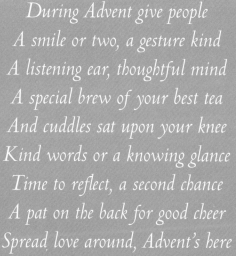

Countdown to Christmas

As we prepare to celebrate the holy birth
Think how you can best remember His name

Praise His name this holy eve
Feel His power and believe

12

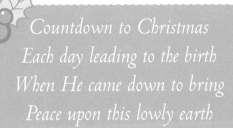

*Countdown to Christmas
Each day leading to the birth
When He came down to bring
Peace upon this lowly earth*

*Listen for the Angels
All singing upon high
Feel love around you
For Christmas is nigh*

*Looking forward
To visiting soon
And to spending
Christmas
With you all*

Christmas is a time to...

Decorate the tree
with tinsel, baubles
and toffees

*Sleep well tonight he's on his way
Close those eyes tight
Listen for his sleigh*

Although I may not tell you
As often as I should
And may not always show you
In every way I could
No one could ever love you
As much as I do
Or care about your happiness
All the year through
Have a wonderful Christmas

The red, red robin is popping in to say
It's not very long now
Until Christmas Day

Jingle bells on Santa's sleigh
Close your eyes in dreams
Listen for them carefully
They're much nearer than they seem

Santa is coming to good girls and boys
With sacks full of happiness
Laughter and joy

Christmas is a time to...

Deck the home with festive cheer

Make sure on
Christmas Eve
You're fast asleep
So Santa Claus
Leaves presents
For you to keep

Christmas weaves a magic spell
For all those who truly believe
Close your eyes and make a wish
For world peace on Christmas Eve

Santa sends his love
Especially to say
Look for a gift
Or two
From
Him
On
Christmas Day

Santa got your message
He said to tell you 'Yes'
What will he bring you?
I think you should guess

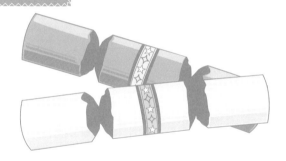

A small choir of angels
Hear the children sing
Dressed as the Nativity
Telling of Christ, the King

Let it snow
On Christmas Eve
A blanket of His love
Covering the earth
So all mankind
BELIEVE

*N*o matter what you believe
Come celebrate this Christmas Eve

All over the world
On this special night
Hearts come together
Because a special light
From a heavenly star
Lead them together
To find a true faith
Lasting forever

HAPPY CHRISTMAS

Christmas Eve, so magical
Songs of praise fill the air
Heralding a true miracle
A world united together
In love, peace and joy

Midnight Mass on Christmas Eve
Feel His loving arms surround you
And then you will truly
BELIEVE

Christmas is a time to...

Listen to sleigh bells on
Christmas Eve

Counting the days to Christmas Eve
When you come to stay with us a while
We have all good things to drink and eat
With festivities planned to make you smile

Come to our party
Bring Christmas cheer
Some food would be handy
And also some beer

Christmas is a time to...

Live, laugh and be merry

Christmas is coming
A time to celebrate
It's Christmas Eve
At our place
It all begins
at 8pm

R.S.V.P.

Christmas is a time to...

Party, party, party

Something is cooking at our house
The table will be laid and fit for a king
Presents are all wrapped and waiting
The Christmas party will be in full swing
The day will be fun-packed and busy
All of the family and friends are due
I have organised all of this festive fun
The last finishing touch will be you

We're having a party but there's a lovely twist
This one's to help Santa fill a small child's list
Be it old or brand new please wrap a small gift
So we can help Santa give a youngster a lift
Please come on over for a time of good cheer
With all of the friends that you hold so dear

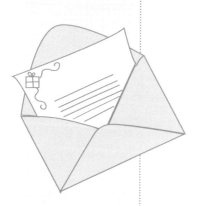

Deer, oh deer
Christmas is very near
Let's get together soon
For good times and cheer

Set your sights on fairy lights
With lots of laughter round the tree
When you join us for a night of fun
At our festive Christmas party
We'll be so pleased to see you
That we can hardly wait
It's not so far away now
What a great way to celebrate

Please drop in here soon
For a toast of good cheer
To the Christmas Holiday
And the upcoming year

Christmas is a time to...

Let your hair down
and have a good time

Do
Join us
To decorate
Our lovely tree
CHRISTMAS
IS FOR SHARING
L
O
V
E
WITH FRIENDS

Happy holiday times
Are meant to be shared
So please come round
And share ours with us

Christmas comes but once a year
And when it does we gather near
To our lovely family and friends
For festive fun that never ends

Come to our Christmas Gathering

The tree is trimmed
The time is right
To gather with friends
This holiday night

Settled in for Christmas
We are in our new home now
Come to our holiday housewarming
The party promises to be such a 'wow'

It's that time of the season
For good friends to get together
Let's party and enjoy
CHRISTMAS

We are having a
HOLIDAY HOUSE WARMING
Please drop in for a glass of good cheer
We can reminisce over the passing year

Christmas is for everyone
Let's party on until it's gone
The place is ours, the time is eight
So hurry round here to celebrate

Christmas is
for Children

Just to say
at Christmas…

This gift comes
with love for a
darling little girl

God grants miracles every day
Celebrate His holy birth
With your own new arrival

Christmas is a time to…

Weave a little magic
into a child's life

Christmas is for Children

Just to say
at Christmas…

A little box of
happiness and joy
for a darling
little boy

May your new child
Be blessed with all good things
At this holy time of the year

Christmas is a time to…

Remember childhood
days and smile

God reminds us every year
To love one another
As we celebrate a new life

Just to say
at Christmas...

Delivered by
Santa with
love from me

Congratulations
On the birth of your child
In this Holy season

Just to say
at Christmas...

Congratulations

on your

child's birth

*S*anta brought you a baby
How wonderful for you

God Bless
Your new child
As your family celebrates
The first Christmas of many

Congratulations on your new arrival
Just in time for the New Year

Just to say,
at Christmas…

Celebrate your
birthday with
angels

God gave you
A special gift
This Christmas
Congratulations
Your daughter is
Beautiful

A baby at Christmas
How perfectly swell
A little Christmas Eve
Or a little sweet Noel

Just to say
at Christmas...

It is a lovely
time to be born,
happy birthday

Christmas, a time of birth
Of hope and of love

Hold me tight on Christmas Eve
Make the special magic stay
Through the joy of Christmas
And each and every day

What a special season, one to enjoy
Especially with your lovely new boy

**Christmas Blessings
To your new family**

For a beautiful baby's first Christmas
This card comes filled with our love
Blessings and joyful good tidings

1st Christmas

The First Christmas was so special
May your first Christmas as parents
Be special too

Just to say
at Christmas…

Nothing makes
Christmas more
special than a
new child in the
family

MAY HE BLESS YOU ON YOUR
1st CHRISTMAS

Christmas is for children
gathered round the tree
One big happy family

Grandparents
For the first time at Christmas
Treasure every second
Of those marvellous
Feelings of love

Just to say
at Christmas…

Nanas like
you are rare,
love you

Congratulations
On becoming
Grandparents
Just in time for
Christmas

Just to say
at Christmas…

I love you lots
Nana and
Grandad

Nana's first Christmas
A feeling so good
To be holding your
GRANDCHILD
Like no-one else could
A treasure so special
Brings joy to your heart
A bond of a special kind
No-one can part

Grandma's first Christmas
A delightful joy to behold
A child sent from heaven
More treasured than gold

Christmas is for Children

God made Christmas more special
When he made you my mummy

I
Love
CHRISTMAS
With sugary sweets
And lollipops, candy canes
And chocolate drops
But I love you
More Mummy
Have a sweet
CHRISTMAS TIME

Mummy & Daddy
I made you a man of snow
But the sun came out
And he had to go

Mummy
I love you and Santa does too
He's bring special treats
For everything you do

Daddy
Sending Christmas kisses
To cover all of your face
For when it comes to dads
You are absolutely ace

A
Christmas
Of love
And
Joy
The perfect time to tell you
That you are truly the best
Mum & Dad
In the world
So glad that
You're mine

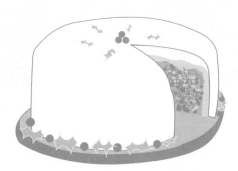

Christmas is a time to...

Leave mince pies out
for your Dad

Daddy you make Christmas so special
I truly love you more every year
You fill the holiday with fun and love
I love every day you spend here

Christmas is for Children

Santa tells me for good girls and boys
He will be bringing a sack full of toys

Ho – Ho – Ho
Christmas Day with snow
Reindeers rest, Santa's the best
Ho – Ho – Ho

Stay chilled this
Christmas

Santa is coming to good girls and boys
With stockings full of chocolates and toys

There's no reindeer ~ only snow!

Funky festive wishes
For the time of your life

May Christmas day be filled with joy
For a special little boy

In
Crinkly paper
All wrapped up in
Ribbons and bows
What will he bring us
Only Santa Claus knows

*S*ending love and Christmas joy
To a special little boy

Christmas kisses and cuddles
For a special little girl

Santa is coming, his sleigh full of toys
He's looking for all the good girls and boys

Christmas is for Children

Mummy and Daddy
I do love you so
I made you this card
Just so you know
Big Christmas kisses
I am sending to you
To tell you thank you
For all that you do

Rudolph found some prickly holly
So Santa do beware
For Rudolph thought it rather jolly
To hide it on your chair

We got a shoebox
To fill with such joy
And sent it to Santa
For a girl or a boy
Who will open it up
On Christmas morn
And then thank Jesus
Because He was born

Santa thought that Rudolph
Deserved a special treat
So he knitted reindeer slippers
To cover up his feet

Christmas is for Children

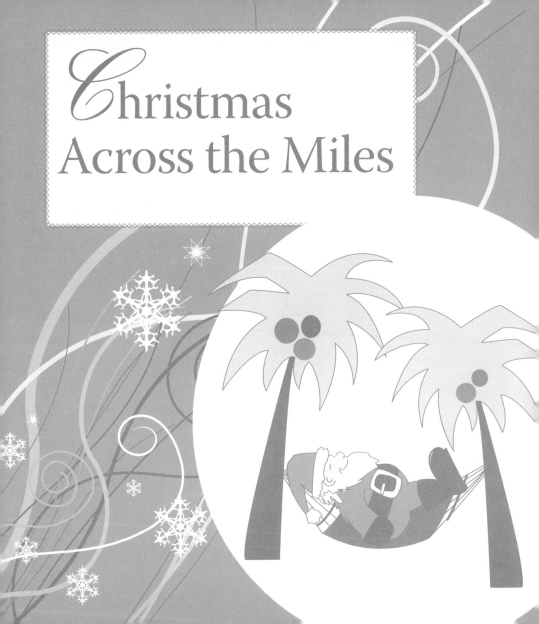

Christmas
Across the Miles

T would follow any star
To be where you are this
Christmas

Christmas is a time to...

*Sit in the sunshine,
dreaming of snow*

*Home is where the heart is
Especially at this festive season
No matter how far you may roam
Come home soon to all of us*

Miles may separate us in body
But nothing can separate us in spirit
May you down a few spirits to celebrate
Our family this Christmas and New Year

Just to say
at Christmas...

My thoughts are
always with you

overseas

I can't fly to see you across the miles
But my heart has wings just to know
You are there somewhere, my love
Thinking of me too at Christmas

Out of sight but always in mind
May you feel my love reaching you
On this lovely Christmas Day

Another year passing by without you
Changing seasons remind me of you daily
Though the miles may seem ever distant
You are always there close to my heart
Every day not only at Christmas

Though miles keep us apart
You are all there in our hearts
From our house to your house
We send you love, peace and joy
For a special Christmas season
As you all celebrate His birth

Across the miles, my love

Every day for me is Christmas
When you hold me close to say
How much you really love me
More and more each day
So darling, do not worry
That we are not together
As every day is special
Our love goes on forever

My wish for Christmas
Is that you return to me safely
In the New Year

Just to say
at Christmas…

You are always
in my thoughts

Darling, sorry you must leave
At this special time of year
But think of all those days ahead
We can fill with festive cheer

Christmas Across the Miles

59

Wishing you were home again
But now it's not too far away
Sending wishes over the miles
With love on Christmas Day

I send a kiss for every mile
That keeps us so far apart
And love to wrap around you
From the bottom of my heart

Merry Christmas, Darling

Sending smiles
Across the miles
Just so we can say
Eat, drink and be merry
Enjoy your Christmas Day

Though I'm not with you
On this special holiday
And miles separate us
Know that in my heart
I am there with you to
Celebrate Christmas

Christmas time is memory time
A perfect time to keep in touch
With friends and family overseas

We may not be together at Christmas
Yet it is still magical just knowing you are there
Feeling it pull us closer together as a family
Over the miles that always keep us apart

Warm wishes from overseas
Sent across the miles to say
We all think of you fondly
On a hot Christmas Day

*S*ending you miles and miles of happy smiles
From all of your loving family overseas

May your first Christmas in
Australia
Be everything you hoped for mate
Glad you came out here to celebrate

Christmas has a magic all of it's own
That brings special memories
Of your family and friends back home

Strolling in the winter sun
Awaiting Christmas Day
May it bring a special magic
To your life in every way

You don't have to come
To the party to be there
And help us give thanks
For all we have in life

I know that wherever you are
And whatever you do, we are
Always in your thoughts
As you are in ours
Our soldier brave
Our dearest son

Thinking of you
Makes the miles disappear,
Linked by thoughts, words unspoken
Enjoying what you like to do, I feel so proud
Christmas thoughts make the smiles appear
For Son, you are missed very much
Now and all year through
God Bless you

May God bless and protect you
At this holy time of year
As all your friends surround you
Bringing endless joy and cheer

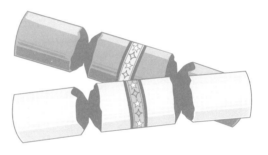

Nothing ever takes the place
Of greetings spoken face to face
Still, thoughts sent in a special card
Renew the love when times are hard
Captures the mood and spans the miles
To take the place of words and smiles
So on this lonely Christmas holiday
My love to you so far away

Christmas Across the Miles

Just to say
at Christmas…

May the New Year
bring you safely
home to us

In this Holiday Season we remember and honour
Those who are no longer with us
And cherish those who are

My
Love
Stand brave, be always true
Know we all depend on you
Enjoy a time of festive cheer
Come home safe to all of us
In the bright New Year

Son, wherever you are at Christmas
In all that you have to do
Know you're always in our thoughts
That we are missing you

Family at
Christmas

To Dad

Just to say
at Christmas…

A 'thank you'
for all you do
for my family

Christmas is a time to…

send loving thoughts
to family and friends

You always made Christmas
Such a wonderful time
For me in childhood
Thank you mum
For treasured
Memories
Of love

Mothers are so special
They make a house a home
Bring laughter to the moments
When you sometimes feel alone
Mum at this special time of year
I would just like to say to you...
I love you so each and every day
For all the things you say and do

You are a really great mum
May Christmas be happy for you

You are one in a million
So special that you shine
I'm proud to be your daughter
Have a joyous time

Mum, you have always made
Our Christmas time together
So very special and magical
Brought a joy to our hearts
Many a smile to our faces
And love to the family home
God bless you for all you do
For being there, for being you

Just to say
at Christmas…

You are the best
mum in all the
world

Family at Christmas

For a great Step-mum
To tell you that I care
Christmas wishes
Sent with my love
So glad you are
Always there

Sending you a special
Christmas time message
As the festive season starts
To say you are loved dearly
You are always in our hearts

Just to say
at Christmas...

You are a lovely
step-mum

Mums
Always make
Christmas
That extra bit special

Deck the halls
Put out the holly
Make this holiday
Happy and jolly

Dad
At Christmas
Miles may keep us apart
But no matter where you are
You are always there in my heart

Just to say
at Christmas…

You are a super
dad all year
through

A
Wish
Especially
For a truly lovely stepfather
Who always gives his time
To make us a happy family
So glad that you are mine
Special Christmas wishes
Love and joy are sent to you
So New Year brings good luck
To make all your dreams come true
Special
Love
X

I saw mummy kissing Santa
Is there something you want
to tell me dad?

Dad you are great
Hope Christmas brings for you
A time to celebrate

Dad
Sending you
My love at Christmas
Because I love you so
I may not always tell you
So I thought you ought to know

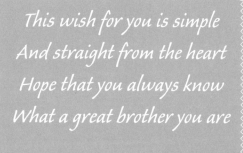

This wish for you is simple
And straight from the heart
Hope that you always know
What a great brother you are

Merry Christmas

Having a brother at Christmas
Is great if you are too little
To open up your own presents

Hey brother,
Wishing you a crazy Christmas
And a truly nauseous New Year

Just to say
at Christmas…

As a brother
you are
number one

I woke up and found you were miles away
My goodness, brother, it must be Christmas
And my wishes have come true

Having a sister at Christmas
Is great, you get the excuse
To play with girls toys

Just to say
at Christmas…

You are my
super sister

You are a beautiful person
A wonderful sister, a lifelong friend
That is what you are to me
Merry Christmas
With love

Christmas has a magic
That gives life a brighter touch
And brings us even closer
To a sister we love so much

You
Are
A very
Special sister
Loved throughout
The year but sending love
Inside this card now that
Christmastime is here
I hope you find the
Things in life that
Will mean the
Most to you
During this
Special
Season

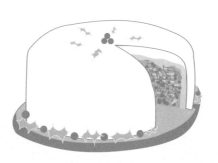

With thoughts of a
Dear sister and brother-in-law
At Christmas more than ever
It is a time to tell you two
We wish the very finest things
In all the world for you

Merry Christmas & Happy New Year

Loving Christmas Wishes

To a special brother and his wife
Whose thoughtfulness
Fills the whole family with love
And brightens this Holy season
With an everlasting joy

A Christmas wish for a
Special brother and sister-in-Law
LOVE - PEACE - JOY
This wishes you all the happiest things
A wonderful season like Christmas brings
Because you are so very special
In all that you say and do
This brings lots of love
Especially for you

Family at Christmas

A loving daughter
Puts the heart into Christmas

Just to say
at Christmas...

You are a
daughter beyond
compare

Daughters
Are made from love
And all things special
They capture your heart
With a smile worth more
Than gold they keep you
Feeling young when you
Get old and they turn
Christmas into a
Magical time

For a wonderful daughter

Thoughts of you make
Christmas
A special season for us
As we celebrate your birth
At this Holy time

This Christmas promises
Memories to treasure
Shared with you
Our daughter we love

Living with you is such bliss
As treasured as a butterfly kiss
I bless the day that you were born
Especially on this Christmas morn

Just to let you know you are always
In many loving thoughts and memories
During each day and throughout the year
But this is especially true at Christmas
Darling, you are such a special son
Merry Christmas

Just to say
at Christmas...

We are so proud
of you, our
darling son

O
Son
You
Are
One
In a
Million
You make
Christmas time
Special and every
Day happy for us
We love you so
Much
Son

Festive fun at Christmas time
For a special boy of mine

For a loving son & his family

Wishing you all a wonderful
Magical Christmas holiday
Just the kind you deserve.

Merry Christmas
with Love

Family ties make
Christmastime more special
Children, parents and
Grandparents
Sharing hopes and memories

Grandpas
Love to snooze
By the Christmas fire
After dinner

A very special
Christmas prayer
That God may grant
to both of you
His blessings for
being such
Amazing
grandparents
Loved with all my
heart

HOLY BIBLE

Nanas
Know how to party
On right down to
The last cracker

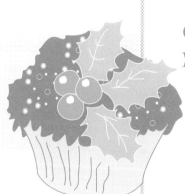

When it comes to Nanas
Or special Christmas days
You really pick up the prize
Nobody compares to you
Or your Christmas treats
At least not in my eyes

Merry Christmas, Nana

Every snowflake is an angel's kiss

Aunties
Always know great
Party games so we
Can all join in the fun

You are a great
Aunt
So glad we are part
Of the same family tree

90

*U*ncles
Do the weirdest
Charade games
They look so funny

Wishing all the happiness
A wonderful Christmas can bring
For an uncle who deserves to have
The very best of everything

Because I love you both
For your caring way
This brings you
Happy wishes
For a merry
Christmas
Day

Without your loving touch and care
Christmas would have no magic
Life would not be so much fun
You make everything so right
And I love you for being
So special in my life
God bless you

May your Christmas Day
Be as special as you are
And may your New Year
Bring good fortune to you

You are a beautiful part of our family
Always, but especially at Christmas
You are lovingly wished all things
To bring you happiness because
Happiness is what you give us
You are part of our very self
And forever in our hearts

Just to say
at Christmas...

Bring joy to
the world in
all you do

Christmas is a time to celebrateLife
And to thank God
For His love

Christmas is a time to...

Marvel at the
miracle of life

O Holy Night

95

C
H
R
I
S
T
MAS
Hear the angels sing
In heaven far above
Heralding the King
Who will fill your hearts
With love

Christmas is a time to...

sing with angels to
celebrate His birth

The greatest gift of all at Christmas
Is God's love for all mankind

A
Day
For us all to
Celebrate His birth
As the church bells chime
And the choir joins in song
May it herald Christmas cheer
That lasts the whole year long
God
Bless

O Holy Night

Starlight, shining bright
Upon us on this holy night
Lead us on and show the way
To serve the Lord every day

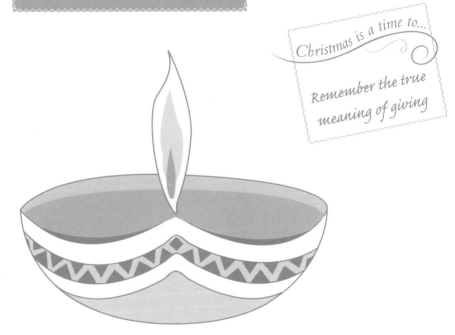

Christmas is a time to...

Remember the true meaning of giving

Listen to the angels sing Celebrating Christ the king

*Forever in our hearts
On this special Christmas Day
Thoughts and memories of you
Will never fade away
God Bless you*

O Holy Night

Feel the joy of Christmas surround you
And thank the Lord for friends and family
Who make the world a brighter place to be

God
Gave
Us
His only Son
He
Gave
Us
His
Love

A
Holy
Event
Wishing you a truly lovely time
At this special time of year
May this Christmas bring
Love, joy & peace
May the New Year
Renew your faith in God
Yourself and your fellow man
So prosperity knocks at your door
Follow
The

*

Christmas is a time to...

Remember the reason
for the season

O Holy Night

May the Kwanzaa celebrations
Renew your faith

As friends and family come together
To celebrate the principles of Kwanzaa
GIVE THANKS TO THE LORD

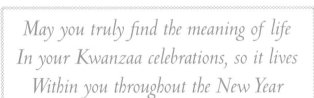

May you truly find the meaning of life
In your Kwanzaa celebrations, so it lives
Within you throughout the New Year

*Here's hoping that Kwanzaa is
A time of happiness
And contentment for you
And your family*

*May good fortune bring your friends and family
Safely to your door at Kwanzaa*

*Kwanzaa, a time to share,
Reflect and renew
Your heritage with
Family and friends*

O Holy Night

May ay you be surrounded by your
loved ones at Kwanzaa

*At this special time of
Kwanzaa
May the love of family and the
Heritage we share
Light the way with happiness
And pride
For many generations to come*

*Let the first fruits of the harvest
Spark a new beginning for you*

Happy Kwanzaa

Let the Nguzo Saba
Guide you and inspire you
Towards greater
Understanding

Let the joy of Umoja fill your heart
As a recommitment of faith.

Happy Kwanzaa

Let the truth and spirit of the season
Stay with you through the year

Happy Kwanzaa

Hanukkah
A good time to thank you
For being all the special things
A friend should be and to tell you
How much our friendship means always

Hope your holiday is wonderful

As you light your Hanukkah candles
Remember old friends and new

Love, peace and joy
Are sent to you for Hanukkah

*B*lessing be upon you at Hanukkah

May Hanukkah bring you
Many happy memories
Of family and friends
Past and present

O Holy Night

You make Hanukkah so special for me
And I hope we spend many more together

Festival of Lights

My dearest friend,
May this Hanukkah
Be an especially
Happy time
For you
And
Yours

Day by day we celebrate the reason
For this truly wonderful season
Happy Hanukkah darling

Hanukkah wishes sent over the sea
Thinking of you at the celebrations
Hope that you are missing me

With warm wishes for you at Hanukkah
May you be blessed with joy, peace
Good health, and all the best things in life

The first candle glows so make a wish
The second radiates with joy and love
The third one gleams with good luck
The fourth is a beam for friendship
The fifth candle is a ray of closeness
The sixth shines with good health
The seventh candle flickers softly
The eighth candle brings peace

As your menorah glows with light
May all eight days be warm and bright

May this season of beauty and light
Fill your heart and home
With happiness
And love

Although you and I believe
In different faiths and miracles
Our hope at these December holidays
Is that we both have joy in our lives,
Love in our hearts and peace in our world.

Have a Happy Hanukkah

It's the Festival of Lights,
May it also be the festival of love,
Closeness, happiness, success, health,
Peace and joy in your world
Now and always

O Holy Night

As Christmas approaches
Think how you can make
The world brighter for those
Who are living in the shadows

Happy is the man who can give
Something that costs nothing
Other than time and love
For his fellow man
Make this year
Special

This Christmas give yourself
To make others happy

*G*ive to those who ask for nothing
But always deserve something

*Live every day as if it was Christmas
Then we will enjoy peace on Earth*

*When Christmas is over
Keep Jesus in mind
Try every day
To be patient and kind*

O Holy Night

Blessings to you and your loved ones
At this holy time of the year

Christmas brings hope
For peace and harmony
With the joy it bestows
Throughout the world

The joy of Christmas on a sunlit morn
Reminiscent of the day He was born
In a land far away they travelled afar
Led by angels and a heavenly star

*S*ilent night, holy night
Pray that world peace comes in sight

Christmas
Is a season of blessings
From Heaven above
A season of sharing
With those we love
A season of caring
Joy and good cheer
And a season of hope
For the coming New Year

Blessings for you and your family
You are remembered with love
At this Holy time of year

O Holy Night

Christmas
Love

Darling, you have made my life complete
And I truly love you so
My love, on our first Christmas together
I hope there are so many more to go

Hold me tight on
Christmas Eve
Make the special
Magic stay
Through the joy
Of Christmas
Until a New Years Day

My
Darling,
Christmastime
A time to say to you
You make my life so magic
With all of the things you do
You have that special way
To fill my life with cheer
Not only at this season
But each day of the year

Christmas Love

You drive me Christmas Crackers
But I'm nuts about you

Christmas is a time to...

Realise that the greatest gift is love

All I want for Christmas
Is you, you, you
To say to me
I do, do, do

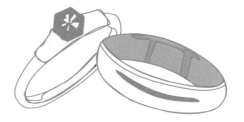

Christmas would not be as magical
Without you, my darling angel

I count the many Christmas Days
During our countless years together
Remember happy times we've shared
And truly hope they last forever

Your smile melts my heart
On this wonderful Christmas
morning

Just to say
at Christmas…

Wrap up your
love in boxes
of joy

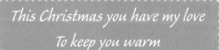

This Christmas you have my love
To keep you warm

Christmas Love 119

My Christmas wish is for you
To know how much happiness
You bring into my life every day
Just simply by being you

Although I may not tell you
As often as I should
And may not always show you
In every way I could
No one could ever love you
Quite as much as I do
Or care about your happiness
All the year through
Have a wonderful Christmas

Just to say at Christmas…
I love you deeply, truly, madly

Christmas is a time to...

Curl up together in front of the fire

Remembering each beautiful moment
That I have spent with you
Every Christmas past and every year anew

You are special to me every day
Not just at Christmas

Christmas Love

Christmas is a time to...

Tell someone special how much you love them

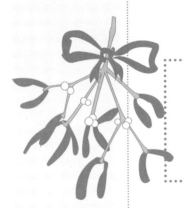

I have a bunch of mistletoe
So come and meet with me
Your kisses are like heaven
So that's where I'd like to be

You know so many ways to make me truly happy
I love you so for each and every one of them

The best Christmas present is
LOVE

Just to say
at Christmas...

You make
every day
special

Every Christmas we
Spend together
I just love you
More and more

Christmas is perfect with you in my life
I will love you forever, my sweet
Darling wife

My
Thoughts are
Always with you
Not just at Christmas
My heart is always yours
Forever and a day

This Christmas I wish
I could find another way to tell you
How much I truly love you
But after all these years together
You will just have to believe me

My Darling
Special loving wishes
Especially at this festive season
But to send my love to you
I do not need a reason

You are such a special person
Someone I'm so glad I met
So here are Christmas wishes
For a day you won't forget

Many thanks for
Everything you do
To make my life so
Wonderful
**Merry Christmas
My darling**

Without you
Christmas would lose
It's magic for me

Especially for you
At Christmas time
With my heartfelt love
And best wishes

Just a little card to tell you
That you are so truly special
To me, in every kind of way
With my wish for happiness
On this Christmas Day

You are my lovely
Christmas Cracker
My heart is full of joy
You are the best girl
In all of the world
And I'm your lucky boy

Just to say
at Christmas...

This gift
comes wrapped
in kisses

Merry Christmas greetings
Are so fondly sent to you
Bringing love and happiness
For everything you do

If my Christmas wishes come true
Then I will spend it all with you

Christmas Love

You are all I want for Christmas
For you make my dreams come true

I love you more than you will ever know
May this Christmas be a special for you
As you make every day for me my love

Just to say
at Christmas...

This gift is
wrapped with
love for you

A box full of love
To bring you such joy
For my favourite girl
From your favourite boy

Opening up my heart
To you at Christmas time
Just to say how much
I truly love you

Just to say
at Christmas...

Feel the
love around you,
capture the
magic

Shine on, my bright star
Lead me to a heavenly place
So safe within your arms
This Christmastime

Christmas Love

My Darling Husband
I love the way you care for me
I love the way you are honest with me
I love the way you brighten up my day
I love the way you make my
Christmas so magical
Most of all, I love you being my husband
Every single day

The wondrous beauty
Of this special season
Captured forever in a
Winter Wedding

Celebrate with us at the most
Wonderful time of the year
At our Winter Wedding
Reserve the date

A fairytale wedding
It this holy Christmas season
Your dreams coming true at last
Two lives, two hearts entwined
Blending friendship with love
That will keep you both warm
And fill your lives with joy
God Bless you both

Join us for
A winter wedding
As we both celebrate
New love, new dreams
A bright new future
As we exchange
Marriage vows

A Winter Wedding
Love fills the moment
Snowflakes fill the air
Saying words of love
Singing words of joy
Warmest Congratulations

Just to say
at Christmas...

I love you more
each day
we share

Christmas is a lovely time
To celebrate marriage vows
May your wedding day
Be truly magical

*No matter what I get for Christmas
You're all I really need*

*Every day, not only at Christmas
You add that sparkle to my life
My sweet and lovely lady
My dearest darling wife*

*Congratulations on your
Christmas Wedding Celebrations
What a lovely time of year
To be celebrating
Your love for each other*

Christmas Love

Each Christmas that I spend with you
Gives me more memories to treasure
Reasons to be happy and content
In our life together as partners

There could not be a better time
To say how much I love you
Or to thank you for the way
You care for me in all you do
Christmas brings a magic glow
The season creates, that's true
But then every day is magical
For me just because of you

Sometimes we are too busy
Keeping up with a hectic life
That I may forget to tell you
I'm so glad you are my wife
So as this Christmas holiday
Happily comes by this way
My New Years resolution is
To tell you every single day

Just to say at Christmas…

I hope you love this token of my love

Darling, sending you
Loving Christmas wishes
To celebrate our 1st Christmas
Together as man and wife

Christmas Love

My   Love
Christmas time is everywhere
Children's laughter, carols fill the air
Promises made, loving words said
Treasured memories in my head
My dearest wish, true love
I pray, comes true
For us upon our
Wedding
Day

Just to say
at Christmas…

You really
mean the world
to me

With love and blessings
Now you are man and wife
May Christmas be special
All through your new life

Not only just in the Christmas season
But also during all the long year through
The love and joy that you give to others
Is the love and joy that comes back to you
This comes with my love, for all that you do
For always being there for me, for being you

On our very first Christmas
In our very own first house
Here is my very first verse
To my very first spouse
Merry Christmas Darling

Christmas Love

Just to say
at Christmas...

I'm loving our
1st Christmas
together
and looking
forward
To many more

A Winter Wedding
As we both celebrate
New love, new dreams
A bright new future
As we exchange
Marriage vows

WARMEST CONGRATULATIONS

Just to say at Christmas…

Loving you is easy because you are my world

Darling, sending you
Loving Christmas wishes
To celebrate our 1st Christmas
Together as man and wife

Christmas Love

139

No matter what I get for Christmas
You're all I really need

Sometimes we are too busy
Keeping up with a hectic life
That I may forget to tell you
I'm so glad you are my wife
So at this Christmas holiday
Happily comes by this way
My New Years resolution is
To tell you every single day

Just to say
at Christmas...

Dreams can
come true,
thanks to you

*Just to say
I'm loving our
1st Christmas together
And looking forward
To many more*

*The Christmas tree Reminds me
How much you Light up my life
For I am such
A very lucky guy*

Christmas Love

Festive
Greetings

MERRY CHRISTMAS
and a
HAPPY NEW YEAR

Christmas is a time to...

Make people smile

Just to say
at Christmas...

Follow your
dreams and they
will come true

Make every day as joyful as Christmas
Love, live and be happy always

Just to say
at Christmas…

Have a fun filled
time and enjoy
yourself

Christmas is a time to…

spread a little magic
all of your own

A wish for all the
Happiness you deserve
At Christmas time
And always

Festive wishes sent to you
In chocolate kisses

Let it snow on Christmas Day

Special seasons greetings
A card full of good cheer
Especially at Christmas
And into the New Year

Christmas is a time to...

Open the chocolates
and know you have
an excuse to
eat them

To a great teacher
Who deserves every
Day of the Christmas
Holidays

Have a peaceful Christmas
And a happy and healthy
New Year

Just to say at Christmas…

Wishing you a truly magical time

When you celebrate Christmas
You celebrate the miracle of life
And the joy of a new beginning
Each New year, so this year make
Every moment of each day count

*H*ope Santa brings you
What you want

Christmas tidings
May it bring you
Great joy

*Wishing you a Christmas
That is bright and happy
Just like you*

*Hope that the holiday brings
surprises, fun and happy things*

*Love and kisses
Christmas wishes
Fondly sent to you*

*Here's a special Christmas message
Carrying a special wish for you
For a truly lovely Christmas
And a Happy New Year too*

*M*ay the merry times of Christmas
Live within you all year long

May you have a wonderful time
At Christmas
And on into the coming
New Year

Santa wishes you both
A Christmas filled
With happiness
Love and joy

Snowflakes fall across the land
Angel kisses soft and white
Shining in the skies above
Stars twinkle in the night
Christmas is magical

This Christmas
Let's hope it's a good one
Filled with good cheer
To herald in a
GREAT NEW YEAR

Deck the halls
Put out the holly
Make this holiday
Happy and jolly

Everything becomes softer
Wonderful and beautiful
Because of the magic wand
That is Christmas

Christmas, a time to reflect
To see what has changed
In your life since last year

HOPE – PEACE – LOVE
The gladness, spirit and essence of
Christmas
Be with you now and always

At this special time
I wish you peace, I wish you
Childhood memories lingering
In the embers of a Christmas
Filled with love and joy

May you feel the loving arms
Of your family and friends
Wrapping around you
This Christmas season

From the moment it begun
I hope this Christmas holiday
Is one that you will remember
As a joyous and happy one

Wishing you a Merry Christmas
Filled with joy and cheer
So that you enjoy each moment
Of the holiday that's here

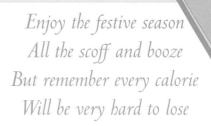

Enjoy the festive season
All the scoff and booze
But remember every calorie
Will be very hard to lose

Special Christmas dishes
May chocolate pass your lips
But remember in the New Year
It will all be there on your hips

Sorry there is no present
To wish you all the best
I gave yours to the charity
Where you sent all the rest
Have A Great Christmas

May Santa's sack
Be full of lovely surprises
Especially for you

Same old socks, soap on a rope
Some presents so awful, it's a joke
Christmas time, mistletoe kisses
May Santa grant all of your wishes

May your Christmas be full of funk and jazz
Designer goods, gadgets and pizzazz

Gather your friends near
Celebrate with Christmas cheer

Reindeers pulling Santa's sleigh
Bringing Christmas joy your way

This Christmas
Spend a little
Laugh a lot
And enjoy

Look at all the Christmas trees
Swaying gently in the breeze
One day each will stand alone
Decorated lovingly in a home

Cheer
Hope
Roses
Icicles
Snow
Treats
Magic
Angels
Special

*If every day was like
Christmas
Then we may have
Peace in the world*

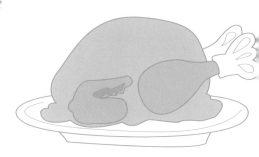

*You are thought of at Christmas
So much more than you know
May your day be filled with love
To keep you warm in the snow*

Christmas is a time to...

*Thank you for
all you do*

*S*pecial thoughts at Christmas
For a day filled with snow

*T*he true meaning of Christmas is LOVE

Hope your Christmas is a cracker

Tinsel, turkey and some
Trimming
Enjoy the day, forget the
Slimming

Have a cracking good Christmas
Full of good cheer
Then start celebrations again
In the New Year

May the holiday
Season
Give you the peace
And joy you deserve

Hope these Christmas vouchers
Come in useful at the sales

Wishing you a designer Christmas
And a New Year full of opportunities

A lot of thought went into this gift
— I knew you would rather
Have the cash to spend yourself!

A beautiful robin
On a winter's day
Tells us that Christmas
Is well on the way

A little red robin is coming to say
He hopes you have fun on
Christmas Day

Sending you sincere wishes
For a fabulous Christmas
Full of fun and laughter

Sending you a huge
Christmas hug

Hope that happiness
Surrounds you
On Christmas Day

May all of your
Christmas wishes
Come true

Merry Christmas greetings
Are so fondly sent to you
Bringing love and happiness
For everything you do

A
Wish
For your
Christmas
To be happy
From the start
With memories
You treasure and
Keep in your heart
H
A
P
P
Y
YULETIDE

A
Very
Merry
Christmas
MY DEAR FRIEND

Wishing you
The best holiday season
EVER

*A wish for Christmas
I send to you
My dear sweet friend
Who is always true*

*Mistletoe and holly
The promise of snow
An aroma of Christmas
The fire all aglow*

*May good friends knock on your door
Bringing good luck and love
Into your life in this
Festive season*

Christmas is a time to...

*Give thanks for
everything in life*

This
Snow
Man
Is
Sending
Good luck
Good cheer
Good health
Good friends

Hope Christmas and New Year is a blast
With fun filled memories that last

*S*ending you a Christmas fairy
To make your dreams come true

*C*hristmas brings out the child in all of us

This year send one card
To all of the office
Just like this one
I am sending to you
And donate the rest
Of your card money
To those who truly need
Christmas cheer

Recycle your cards each Christmas
Show the world you care

Special words at Christmas
Are more precious than a present

Kind words cost
Nothing
Yet make Christmas
Magical

Christmas is a time to...

Be grateful for
life's rich tapestry

The most perfect Christmas gift
Does not cost you money
It comes from the heart
The gift of love

Special thoughts at Christmas
For a fun, festive time

Christmas is here, a time to say
Have a truly uplifting, magical day

A warm wish, especially for you
At Christmas

May every single moment of your
Christmas
Be filled with joy and happiness

Faces lit with wonderment and joy
They loved all of your kind gifts
Children make Christmas
Enclosed are photos
Sent with our love

Christmas Memories
Each one treasured
Forever in your heart
A snapshot of a time
Of celebration & love

Festive fun is coming your way
To make it a perfect Christmas Day

Happy
New Year

Christmas is a time to...

Anticipate a bright
New Year

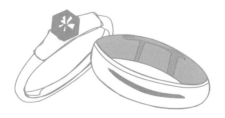

*C*hristmas brings a special kind of love
That sees us married in the New Year

Happy New Year

Off with the old and bring in the new
May good fortune and happiness
Come especially to you
This New Year

Wine me, dine me, Christmas time me
Fill all of my holiday with cheer
Take me on a journey into the
New Year

Christmas is a time to...

Eat until you feel fit to diet in the New Year

May the New Year
Chase away last year's blues
And take you on the path you choose
Bringing you good cheer

Sending my warmest wishes
For the coming New Year

Looking forward to a year that's new
And filled with moments spent with you

New Year
New beginnings and adventures
New hopes and dreams
New You

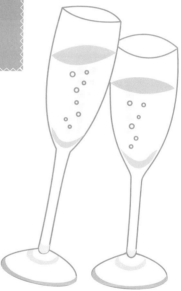

A bubbly Christmas
And a New Year full of fizz
HAPPY NEW YEAR

*N*ew Year blessings
To you and your lovely family

Enjoy your holiday with all good cheer
And welcome in a bright New Year

Raise a glass of good cheer
To herald in a great New Year

Warmest greetings for festive cheer
May good luck bring in your New Year

Happy New Year

At Christmas I give you my heart
Looking forward to the New Year
When we both finally tie the knot
So that I can give you my name too

It's now
A New Year
New adventures
New resolutions
New challenges
New thoughts
New ideas
New you
New
me

May the New Year
Bring you joy and happiness

*C*hristmas sparkle for a magical
New Year

May the lovely festive cheer
Herald in a great
NEW YEAR

Happy New Year

177

*Another
New Year
Same old, same old
Make this year different
Make it count*

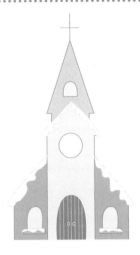

*What are you
Giving God
This Christmas and New Year*

*R*emembering loved ones and friends
At Christmas and into the New Year

New Year's Eve
A time to reflect on
Treasured memories

As we sit here in the sun
Contemplating festive fun
We send our thoughts of love to you
For a great New Year in all you do

Happy New Year

*L*ead heavenly star
Unto a bright New Year

Merry Christmas greetings
Are so fondly sent to you
Bringing love and happiness
For everything you do

For all the help you gave
Throughout the past year
Sending heartfelt thanks

Mum, may you find happiness in every day
Of the New Year that's coming this way

See the red, red robin
Bringing winter cheer
Hopping into Christmas
And a bright New Year

As one year ends and another draws near
May you look back on treasured times
And forward to new adventures

Happy New Year

May the New Year bring you a happiness
That you truly deserve, my dear friend

This Christmas and New Year
Give everyone that you meet
A special gift to remember
That will cost you nothing
And may mean everything
— a simple smile

Take time to smell the Christmas cheer
And relax in anticipation of the New Year

*L*ooking ahead to a bright
New Year

Christmas, a time of great reflection
Before a New Year dawns

Happy New Year

My New Year's resolution is...

To throw away clothes before I buy new
And to spoil someone special
(that one being you)

Tell me, what is yours for this year?

Christmas is a time to...

Make plans for a brighter tomorrow

My New Year's resolution is...

To love more, to live more
To earn more, to give more

Tell me, what is yours for this year?

May this New Year's resolution
Last throughout the year

New Year - New diet - New you

My New Year's resolution is...

To try to diet, to try to save
To try to be quiet, to try to behave

Tell me, what is yours for this year?

Happy New Year

The champagne is now chilling
So we hope that you are willing
To be our special guest
At our New Year's Eve fest

Christmas is a time to...

Let go of the past and plan for the future

Don't party too much at Christmas
Save yourself for our New Year's Eve party

Bid fond farewell to the year that's gone
Come round to ours and party on

May the New Year
Bring changes in your life
That make you smile

*N*ew Year
A time to leave behind old memories
And to create new ones

Happy New Year

Suppliers

UK Wholesalers

Crafts Too Ltd
Unit 2 Kingstons Industrial Estate
Eastern Road
Aldershot
Hants GU12 4YA
Tel: (+44) (0)1252 330024
www.crafts-too.com
Wholesaler of craft products importing and distributing ranges from USA & Europe

Design Objectives
www.docrafts.co.uk
Contact them directly through the website or contact Magna Craft on 01730 815555

Personal Impressions
Curzon Road
Chiltern Industrial Estate
Sudbury
Suffolk CO10 2XW
Tel: (+44) (0)1787 375241
www.richstamp.co.uk
Visit website or call for your nearest stockists of their craft products from USA & UK. Importers of products listed in USA section

Pergamano UK
Curzon Road
Chiltern Industrial Estate
Sudbury
Suffolk CO10 2XW
Tel: (+44) (0)1787 375241
www.richstamp.co.uk
Sole UK importer of Pergamano Parchment Craft Products. Contact for your nearest Pergamano tutor and retailer

UK Retailers

Witzend Arts & Crafts
Witzend
25 Cookesmere Lane
Sandbach
Cheshire CW11 1BQ
www.buycraftsonline.co.uk
Online art and craft retailer specialising in card making – sorry no personal callers. Retailers of products from Personal Impressions and Pergamano UK

Craft Creations
Ingersoll House
Delamere Road
Cheshunt
Hertfordshire
EN8 9HD
Tel: (+44) (0)1992 781900
www.craftcreations.co.uk
Greeting card blanks and general craft retailer. Mail order or contact for stockists

Craftwork Cards Ltd
Unit 2, The Moorings
Waterside Road
Stourton
Leeds
West Yorkshire
LS10 1RW
Tel: 0113 276 5713
www.craftworkcards.com
Sell greetings cards blanks and other specialist card making materials. Mail order available, but visit the shop for the full range of supplies

Fred Aldous Ltd
37 Lever Street
Manchester
M1 1LW
Tel: (+44) (0)161 326 4224
www.fredaldous.co.uk
*Originally established in 1886,
this is an Aladdin's Cave of art
and craft materials with craft
workshops available there too*

Hobbycraft Stores
Tel: 0800 027 2387
www.hobbycraft.co.uk
*General craft retailer
countrywide. Mail order
available or call for your
nearest store*

Paper Cellar Ltd
Langley Place
99 Langley Road
Watford
Hertfordshire
WD17 4AU
Tel: 0871 871 3711
www.papercellar.com
*Specialize in paper products,
including card making
materials. Buy online or visit
website for nearest stockist*

USA

The ranges of craft products
listed here are imported into the
UK by Personal Impressions see
the UK listing for contact details

American Traditional Designs
442 First NH Turnpike.
Northwood
NH 03261
Tel: 1-800-448-6656
www.americantraditional.com
*Embossing stencil manufacturers.
Visit the website for details of
products and local stockists*

Artistic Wire Limited
752 North Larch Avenue
Elmhurst
IL 60126
Tel: 630-530-7567
www.artisticwire.com
*View a full range of wires and
accessories and locate your
nearest stockist from the website*

Art Institute Glitter, Inc.
712 N Balboa Street
Cottonwood
Arizona
86326
Tel: toll free 877-909-0805
www.artglitter.com
*Projects, products and a gallery
online with details of suppliers
in your area*

Magic Mesh
PO Box 8
Lake City
MN55041
Tel: 651-345-6374
www.magicmesh.com
*Full range of products, project
ideas for card making and
scrapbooking, with stockist list*

Ranger Industries Inc
15 Park Road
Tinton Falls
NJ 07724
Tel: 732-389-3535
www.rangerink.com
*Visit website to see vast range of
products for rubber stamping*

Suppliers

Tsukineko, Inc
17640 NE 65th Street
Redmond, WA 98052 USA
Tel: (425) 883-7733
www.tsukineko.com
Manufacturers of unique ink products and craft accessories that fire your imagination

Uchida Of America, Corp.
3535 Del Amo Boulevard
Torrance
CA 90503
Tel: 1-800-541-5877
www.uchida.com
Manufacturers of art and craft materials for card making, scrapbooking and art projects

USArtQuest Inc
7800 Ann Arbor Road
Grass Lake
MI 49240
Tel: 800-766-0728
www.usartquest.com
Visit the website for tips and techniques to help you with your arts and crafts projects

Europe

Kars Creative Wholesale
Industriweg 27
Industrieterrein 'De Heuning'
Postbus 97
4050 EB Ochten
The Netherlands
Tel: (+31) (0) 344 642864
www.kars.nl
Visit website or call for your nearest stockists of Pergamano and other craft products

JEJE Produkt V.O.F.
Verlengde Zuiderloswal 12
1216 BX Hilversum
The Netherlands
Tel: 035 624 6732
www.jejeprodukt.nl
Suppliers of Sandy Art product range, stickers and ahesive products

Pergamano International
Postbus 86
1420 AB Uithoorn
The Netherlands
Tel: (+31) (0) 297 526256
www.pergamano.com
Parchment craft manufacturers. Visit website for product information or nearest stockists

Australia

ParchCraft Australia
PO Box 1026
Elizabeth Vale
South Australia 5112
www.parchcraftaustralia.com
View metal parchment craft tools on website

Canada

Magenta Rubber Stamps
2275 Bombbardier Street
Sainte-Julie
Quebec J3H 3B4
Tel: 450-922-5253
www.magentastyle.com

South Africa

Brasch Hobby
10 Loveday Street South
Selby
Johannesburg
South Africa 2001
Tel: +27 11 493 9100
www.brasch.co.za
*Manufacturers and distributors of genuine
heritage craft products*

About the Author
Judith Wibberley

Born and bred in Cheshire, Judith moved to Manchester
when she married her husband, Colin. After raising their
children, James and Deborah, she opened an Arts & Crafts
Centre specialising in hand made cards where her love
of creative writing lead to these verses especially for card
makers. Although she will always be a northern lass, Judith
now resides in the beautiful Otter Valley in Devon, where she
writes for crafters and children. She has her own website for
crafters and writers at www.judithwibberley.co.uk.

Index